SYDNEY SKETCHBOOK

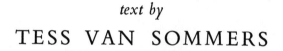

text by

TESS VAN SOMMERS

drawings by

UNK WHITE

RIGBY

RIGBY PUBLISHERS LIMITED • ADELAIDE
SYDNEY • MELBOURNE • BRISBANE
NEW YORK • LONDON

First published October 1965
Reprinted December 1965
Reprinted October 1966
Reprinted April 1967
Reprinted January 1968
Reprinted May 1971
Reprinted January 1973
Reprinted September 1974
Revised edition published September 1981
Copyright © Tess van Sommers and Unk White 1965
ISBN 0 85179 528 5
Printed in Hong Kong

CONTENTS

MACQUARIE LIGHTHOUSE

The little boat dipped and rolled in the swell off South Head, and the man in the stern scowled as he squinted at the top of the cliffs. Francis Greenway, convict and architect, was taking one of his regular looks from the sea at the building of the lighthouse Governor Macquarie had ordered him to design. Nothing was going well with the work. The Governor, who had laid the foundation stone of the tower in July 1816, had expected the job to be finished in nine months. It was now in its second year.

Mr Greenway disliked having to use soft sandstone quarried on the site. He said it would not last, and he was right. Within fifty years the tower had to be reinforced with iron. By 1883 the whole elegant structure had been condemned. But the lighthouse had served well. It replaced the crude system of bonfires that had been lit on the headland, and won Greenway his emancipation. In December 1817 Governor Macquarie made up a breakfast party to drive out and inspect the completed work. He was so delighted with "this noble magnificent edifice" that he gave Greenway his conditional pardon.

Greenway had been dead more than forty years when they tore down the crumbling lighthouse and put up the one that now stands alongside the original site. The late Victorians paid him the compliment of copying the general outline of his creation for the new building. But Greenway never cared for plagiarism; no doubt he would have found fault with the replacement.

When the lamps in the original lighthouse were first lit they "astonished a mariner when he beheld them from thirty-eight miles out at sea." The second light can, officially, be seen twenty-five miles off shore.

4

THE OLD MINT

Governor Macquarie's critics never ceased pointing out that he had virtually paid in rum for Sydney's second general hospital. Looking back, it seems a brilliant stroke by the Governor to have acquired a huge public building for nothing, whatever the means employed.

The first general hospital was in what is now Lower George Street. By Macquarie's time it was a filthy house of death. The Governor then let the contract for a new one in Macquarie Street to three men who had never built anything —D'Arcy Wentworth, Garnham Blaxcell, Alexander Riley. In return they were permitted to import 45,000 gallons of rum in three years. This was almost a monopoly, but the three speculators do not seem to have made much profit on it.

The hospital, the first part of which was opened in 1816, was in three sections. The present Sydney Hospital stands on the site of the large central block, which was pulled down in 1879. To the north and south of the main block were separate wings—surgeons' quarters. The wing in the north still stands, as part of Parliament House. Behind it a mess of additions has given way to modern quarters for the MPs. Its twin, the southern building, which first housed the assistant surgeons, stands serenely near the top of Macquarie Street, its pillared façade admired as a fine relic of colonial design.

From 1885 to 1926 a branch of the Royal Mint worked there, producing the first New South Wales sovereigns, beloved by collectors. Until the late 1970s it housed various government departments. It then began to be renovated as a State museum of social and cultural history specialising in stamps, coins, and the development of our early coinage.

6

CADMAN'S COTTAGE

This, the oldest dwelling in the City of Sydney, nestling behind the great ocean terminal at Circular Quay, was built in 1815 to house the coxswains of government boats. Though rather grandly called a barrack and built in stone under the direction of no less than Francis Greenway, it was (and is) a humble place of four rooms.

John Cadman, a West Countryman who had been transported for stealing a horse, was holding a conditional pardon and had become assistant government coxswain when the barrack was put up. It is not certain that he lived there for any length of time in the first years. But after he rose to be Superintendant of Boats he took over the place as his perquisite and it was his home for fifteen years with the ex-convict woman he married in his old age (she had been sent out for stealing a hairbrush).

Soon Sydneysiders forgot to talk of the Coxswain Barrack and spoke of "Cadman's Cottage". He was a public figure, constantly on view as he supervised the launching and hauling up, on the small beach in front of the cottage, of the boats in which he and his crews carried officials, including the Governor, up and down the harbour and as far away as Parramatta.

Cadman retired in his seventies, one-eyed and cantankerous, to become an innkeeper. The cottage passed to the Water Police. Then, when the Sailors' Home was opened alongside in 1865, it served as an annexe to it.

It was rescued from its mean estate in the early 1970s by the Sydney Cove Redevelopment Authority and the National Parks and Wildlife Service, and restored as nearly as possible to what it must have looked like in Cadman's time. Today it is part museum, part book and souvenir shop.

ST ANDREW'S CATHEDRAL

As early as 1812, Governor Macquarie, noble dreamer, decided to give Sydney Town a cathedral suitable for a city. Four years later, convict architect Greenway, his imagination ever bounding forward into grandeur, produced plans. They would have graced any thriving community, let alone an unhappy huddle of convicts and keepers on an inhospitable shore. Greenway's Metropolitan Church, St Andrew's, was to be set in a sweep of gardens, with, near by, a bishop's palace, divinity school, museum, and library. Governor and architect gloated over the concept. In 1817 Macquarie laid the foundation stone.

Work had hardly begun when Commissioner Bigge arrived, crying halt. Sent to investigate rumours of Macquarie's ambition and extravagance, he was outraged by the idea of the cathedral. What the colony really needed, he said, was another gaol.

Eighteen years later, Governor Bourke relaid Macquarie's stone, and his architect, James Hume, went to work. But lack of funds halted the building. A temporary weatherboard structure had to be used. Then, in 1847, Edmund Thomas Blacket, new Colonial Architect, redesigned St Andrew's to be what a contemporary unjustly called "the least interesting Gothic cathedral in the world." By the time it was finished in 1874 careless street planning had hemmed in the front entrance; at the other end, George Street ran within a few feet of the eastern elevation. It was necessary to reverse the position of the altar, seal the great western doors, and allow the congregation in by side and rear entrances.

Bishop and pawn, the back-to-front cathedral and its diocesan registry, squat like oversized pieces on undersized squares, pinned down by a great ugly queen, the Town Hall.

HYDE PARK BARRACKS

The Male Convict Barracks, begun in 1817 on the eastern side of what is now Queen's Square, and finished the following year, were built to house up to a thousand felons in large dormitories. This was Macquarie's scheme for ridding the town of gangs of convicts turned loose at night. After their day's labour on government works they slept where they could, an extraordinary system that led to robbery and violence; some of the convicts even used to hire pistols for a night's marauding.

Greenway's three-storied barracks are one of his best works. The *Sydney Gazette* of the day called it ''a noble structure . . . executed conformably with the most elegant proportions of the Greek school.'' Governor Macquarie was so pleased that he gave Greenway his full pardon. He arranged for the building to have a handsome clock—since replaced— and gave the craftsman who made it a grant of 500 acres.

From the 1840s to the 1880s the main part of the barracks was used to lodge newly arrived immigrant women from the British Isles. A District Court was squeezed into one corner, and room was later made for an Institution for Aged Females.

Eventually law officers took over the whole building and set about vandalising it by tacking on a hideous jumble of out-houses. At the end of the 1970s these eyesores were cleared away and work began on turning the barracks into a State museum of history. Amid the general approval only one argument arose: should the post-Greenway palm tree in front of the building remain? The Noes had a strong case.

CONSERVATORIUM OF MUSIC

Of all Governor Macquarie's works the one that inflamed his adversaries most was the building put up as stables for his horses and quarters for his servants.

Macquarie, housed in damp, decaying old Government House in Bridge Street, complained that "no private gentleman in the colony is so ill-accommodated as I am." In 1817 he sent Francis Greenway directions to draw up plans for stables for thirty horses and a "handsome and commodious castellated house" for the residence of the Governor.

But then the Home Government vetoed any new vice-regal residence in the near-bankrupt colony. Greenway was allowed to go ahead with the stables only. Macquarie ordered these to be of brick, inexpensive, and run up in three months. It has been said that he was alarmed and dismayed when he found that what his new civil architect actually was giving him were handsome, commodious, castellated stables. Why, if this were so, he did not have the work halted is not explained.

Greenway's motive for seemingly disregarding orders is also a mystery. Did he and the Governor, with their joint passion for splendid architecture, hope that the stables would set the tone for an even grander Government House, to be built in spite of the croakers in London? Whatever the truth, the stables scandalized the colonists and threw Commissioner Bigge into a frenzy over the "useless magnificence" of the building.

At first it was used as vice-regal stables, and at one stage it even housed the mounts of a Hunt Club. Then the courtyard was roofed—in a totally different architectural style—and in 1916 the Governor's Folly became the State Conservatorium of Music.

ST JAMES' CHURCH

In 1828 the fashionable parishioners of St James' Anglican Church, near Hyde Park, saw nothing humorous about the events of Sunday, 6 July. The bell had scarcely ceased ringing when a commotion began. Wild Mr Edward Hall, editor of the *Monitor* newspaper, was rattling at the door of his high-sided pew, while his motherless young daughters looked on in fright.

Mr Hall, who had come to Sydney as a free settler, spent a lot of his time in gaol for libelling the authorities. He'd been employing a recent stretch of freedom by attacking the pastor of St James', Archdeacon Thomas Hobbes Scott. Now the Archdeacon had retaliated by locking him out of his pew. Hall did not hesitate. "Leaping like a kangaroo," as he later boasted, he went over the top, burst the pew door, and hustled his brood to their seats.

The following Sunday three beadles were standing guard at the pew, staves at the ready. Hall sat himself and his daughters on the stone altar steps. Divine service proceeded, the congregation rustling with shock. But Archdeacon Scott, a former wine merchant whom some suspected of hastening into holy orders so he could take up the rich living of St James', won the battle. He boarded up the pew "like the deck of a ship." He and the fighting editor then waged a long, inconclusive battle in the courts.

Francis Greenway, who had designed St James' in 1819 as a courthouse, had been livid when Commissioner Bigge made him convert it into a substitute for the cathedral he and Governor Macquarie were planning. "Methodist chapel!" he grumbled as he went about the conversion. But today we admire the church for its Georgian grace. It has been much restored, from its copper-sheathed bell-tower to the sandstone foundations, and always with a faultless sense of period.

ST MARY'S CATHEDRAL

The dramatic beginnings of Roman Catholicism in Australia lie on Church Hill. Where St Patrick's College stands, next to the old church of the same name, was the cottage of ex-convict William Davis, Irish rebel. For two years, in 1818-20, he secretly sheltered the Sacrament consecrated by a priest deported from New South Wales for saying Mass without permission. There had been Roman Catholics in New South Wales from the time of the First Fleet, but their religion was proscribed. They were obliged, on penalty of floggings for absenteeism, to attend Protestant services. The hidden Sacrament on Church Hill kept hope alive at a time when the feeling of persecution was intense.

Governor Macquarie had deported the unauthorized Father Jeremiah Flynn as he feared that a "designing artful priest" might stir up a spirit of resentment among the Irish in the colony. But it was Macquarie who, three years later, magnanimously laid the foundation stone of St Mary's Chapel, the first Roman Catholic church in Australia. This was on the site where the great basilica now stands, opposite Hyde Park. Macquarie, a Mason of many years' standing, made a neat joke about the fact after he had trowelled the stone into place.

St Mary's became a cathedral after the first Bishop, Dr Polding, arrived in 1835. The enlarged austere Gothic building burnt down in 1865, and the temporary wooden church that took its place was also destroyed by fire.

Another wooden pro-cathedral was then built and was used until the first part of William Wardell's great Perpendicular Gothic cathedral could be opened in 1882. Work went on until 1928, but the cathedral is unfinished. It still lacks the twin spires that were planned for it.

18

VAUCLUSE HOUSE

Sir Henry kissed, Sir Henry kissed, Sir Henry kissed the Quaker.
And what if he did? You ugly thing, I'm sure he did not ate her.
So sang the wags of Sydney, and no doubt ebullient Sir Henry
Brown Hayes, too, roared out the lampoon. This naughty
knight, formerly sheriff of Cork, transported for abducting a
Quaker heiress, did not behave like a convict. He set about
making himself comfortable. In 1803 he created what was
described as a "rustic little paradise" on about 100 acres of
Crown land near Watson's Bay, naming his estate Vaucluse.

But there were serpents in his Eden. It was plagued with
snakes. So he imported forty barrels of genuine Irish bog, and
had convicts of Irish birth dig it into a trench around his
house, while he spurred them on by singing songs in praise of
St Patrick's power over vipers. According to legend, the
snakes quit.

After Sir Henry came Captain John Piper, Controller of
Customs, but his tenancy was brief. When he was suspended
from his post in 1827 he sold Vaucluse and its land to William
Charles Wentworth. Building on Hayes' beginnings, which
he described as "a very uncomfortable residence," Wentworth housed himself in a fashion that suited his dignity as
statesman, lawyer and newspaper pioneer.

In 1910 Vaucluse House passed from Wentworth's des-
cendants into State ownership, and seventy years later came
under the Historic Houses Trust of New South Wales.
Visitors may dawdle among relics of Wentworth's grandeur,
including the floor tiles he imported from Pompeii and the
sole chair left there from his elaborate dining-room suite
which came from the Doge's Palace in Venice.

DARLINGHURST GAOL

When the prisoners marched in chains from the decaying prison in George Street to the big new gaol at Darlinghurst in 1841 the people stood in the streets and jeered. There were 159 felons in the cavalcade, 119 men and 40 women. Three years later a crowd of ten thousand milled outside the gaol's great stone wall to watch murderer John Knatchbull hang on the public gallows. Until 1852 all hangings were public. The last hanging at the gaol was in 1907, of the sixty-seventh prisoner to die on the gallows there.

The new prison for which Commissioner Bigge had called, planned in 1835, was a long time building. Thirteen years earlier, convicts had begun to dig stone for its wall on Goat Island and in the Woolloomooloo quarries. Some of the marks they carved in the blocks, so that a tally could be kept of their quota of cut stone, are still legible.

The gaol was planned by Mortimer Lewis, on an American model, as a series of curved buildings grouped around a chapel. In 1840, a time of depression, free labour was used on the chief gaoler's house and two cell wings under a scheme to ease "the great destitution among the working classes." Strenuous but not always successful efforts were made to extract useful work from the prisoners, who worked at trades seven hours a day. Discipline was severe. One of the few amenities was the fact that no cell had a ceiling less than ten feet high. In World War I, German prisoners-of-war were housed in the gaol, and Long Bay took over the criminals. In 1921 the massive buildings threw off their ugly past. Shorn of its penal trappings, Darlinghurst Gaol opened its gates to hopeful youth and became East Sydney Technical College.

ELIZABETH BAY HOUSE

"A few days ago I saw one of the most perfect places I ever saw in my life," Mrs Robert Lowe wrote to her mother in 1842. "The drive to the house is cut through rocks covered with the splendid wild shrubs and flowers of this country. Here and there an immense primeval tree. The house is built of white stone and looks like a nobleman's place. In the garden are the plants of every climate from Rio to the West and East Indies, China and even England. Bulbs from the Cape and beautiful roses are to be seen. Oranges, lemons, citrons, guavas and pomegranates are in full bloom."

But there were drawbacks to the garden of Elizabeth Bay House, home of Alexander Macleay, Colonial Secretary of New South Wales, as seen through the eyes of an English-woman accustomed to soft greenness. It was too dry; the plants grew out of sandy white soil. "A few English showers," she observed, "would improve it."

Macleay's lovely domain of 54 acres was the wonder of the colony. The land had come to him in 1828 as a grant from Governor Darling, who respected his knowledge as a natural-ist and horticulturist. Macleay completed Elizabeth Bay House in 1837, but lived there only nine years. His heirs used pistols and bloodhounds to guard the treasures of the garden against despoilers. But in the long run there was no defence against land hunger. A great slice of the garden was sold in 1875; the rest of the estate was cut up in 1927.

In 1941 the Palladian mansion was converted into a patch-work of fifteen flats. By a miracle the magnificent curved staircase remained unharmed. It was an inspiration to the restorers who put the place in order after its purchase by the State Government. Exquisitely decorated as it was in its hey-day as a private home, the house is open to visitors and for ex-hibitions.

DARLINGHURST COURTHOUSE

Fittingly for a penal colony, criminal court work began promptly in New South Wales. On 11 February 1788 two convicts were convicted of stealing, one being sentenced to 150 lashes, the other to be marooned on Rock Island (later called Pinchgut). The first civil action was brought by convicts against the captain of a transport, whom they accused of stealing belongings they had given him for safekeeping. He was found guilty. In September 1795, during Governor Hunter's term, there was another strange civil case. Two soldiers of the New South Wales Corps were sued for £500 damages for shooting a prize pig. To the astonishment of the colony the soldiers were ordered to pay 20/- each.

The courts were shuffled from one place to another until Greenway's building in King Street, the first Supreme Court, was ready. Meddling Commissioner Bigge had forced Greenway to turn his original courthouse into St James' Church. The peppery little architect was deeply dissatisfied with the makeshift he then had to create alongside the church to serve as courts. The building, not opened until 1828, handled civil and criminal cases until the new Criminal Court was built at Darlinghurst fourteen years later.

Some grumbling was heard from lawyers about having to travel to work as far as Darlinghurst. But on the whole Sydney was pleased with the fine Greek-Doric building designed by Mortimer Lewis, which has worn wonderfully well. At the time it was regarded as a stroke of inspiration to build the new courthouse hard up against the back of Darlinghurst Gaol. As one newspaper put it, this arrangement would "obviate the lamentable exhibition of prisoners parading through the town to the courthouse for trials, and risk of their escape."

THE GARRISON CHURCH

When William Grant Broughton, only Bishop of Australia, called a parish meeting in old St Phillip's Church, on Church Hill, in December 1839, he had a pressing problem. St Phillip's was overcrowded; a church must be built on Miller's Point to take the overflow. The Rocks area of the Point swarmed with sailors, not a church-going breed. The Bishop had them in mind when he addressed his parish officers— the new church, Holy Trinity, was to be for mariners.

But Holy Trinity became primarily a soldiers' church. In 1843 services began in the part-finished building, designed by Henry Ginn. Redcoats stationed at Dawes Point regularly attended the morning service. So Holy Trinity became the first Garrison Church, and until 1870, when the British Government withdrew Imperial troops from the colony, soldiers of famous regiments—replicas of whose insignia and crests were set up in it not long ago—were regular attendants. In the 1860s the rector was paid 10s. a head per year for every Church of England soldier at the Dawes Point Battery whose family he visited weekly—limit 100 men on this allowance.

Holy Trinity was enlarged to Gothic designs by Edmund Blacket. The elegance this lent to what had been a ramshackle building stimulated gifts, notably a rich east window, a memorial to the grandparents of David Scott Mitchell.

The Garrison Church has two curious features in its history. One is that for thirty years no collection plate was passed around, offerings being taken at the door. The other is that the church was never consecrated. Holy Trinity is now tenderly preserved as an historical monument as well as a parish church. It has a regular Sunday congregation, and is always packed when the anniversary of the laying of the foundation stone on 23 June 1840 is commemorated.

ADMIRALTY HOUSE

This handsome colonnaded stone building, which with its splendid gardens dominates Kirribilli Point, has since 1916 been the Sydney residence of Australia's Governor-General. The house was bought in 1885 by the State of New South Wales as a residence for the Naval Commander-in-Chief. About a decade earlier the house had been described at an auction as having "a wide verandah, a spacious entrance hall, drawing and dining rooms, 10 bedrooms, and the usual rooms in the main part of the house; a large courtyard, servants' rooms, kitchen, stables, etc., with an abundant water supply, which never failed in the driest weather."

To make this residence fit for British admirals, the State enlarged the house to its present grand proportions. It therefore came like a thunderclap to the State authorities when the second last admiral to use it, Sir George King-Hall, struck his flag there and handed the residence over to the Commonwealth!

Indignantly, the State pointed out that Admiralty House was its property. But it took seventeen years of argument and a High Court suit to decide in the State's favour. The Commonwealth did not lawfully own the House until 1948, when, at last, it acquired the property through a Crown grant.

When the Governor-General is in residence citizens are free to visit the police office at the gates of the house and sign the Visitors' Book, but relatively few are invited into its elegant rooms or asked to stroll the lawns at garden parties. For the rest, it is possible to admire the immaculate grounds from a passing ferry.

The row of old stone buildings along the waterfront of Admiralty House is all that remains of a fortification placed there in 1885 to support the guns of Pinchgut.

THE AUSTRALIAN MUSEUM

Alexander Macleay, Colonial Secretary, has often been called founder of the Australian Museum, but it was the Earl of Bathurst who told Governor Darling to establish a Colonial Museum. The beginnings of the collection (mainly specimens of birds and animals, aboriginal artifacts, and curiosities) were lodged wherever room could be found—in State legal offices, in the old Post Office in Bent Street, even in Darlinghurst Courthouse. Convicts were employed specimen-hunting. For some years the collection was in charge of a transportee. He found favour with Macleay, first chairman and most active early patron of the museum, but was unpopular with other officials, some of whom called him a "damned bird skinner" and "rascally bird stuffer."

The first permanent building (with modern additions in the same fine sandstone, it stands on the corner of College Street) was begun in 1846. Work dragged on until 1867, to a chorus of grumbling about expense and the unsightliness of the unfinished buildings. The collections were moved from Darlinghurst in 1849, but the museum was still not taken seriously. As soon as the exhibition hall was finished it was used as a public hall.

At first, in its anxiety to collect, the museum accepted almost anything. There was even a collection of plaster casts taken from the faces of the worst criminals in the colony after execution, part of the stone desk on which Martin Luther translated the Bible, and a "remarkable radish root grown in the form of a human hand."

Among past directors, Gerard Krefft, whose term was in the 1860s-70s, named the Queensland Lung-fish, and quarrelled violently with the trustees. When sacked, he locked himself in his room and had to be carried out into the street, chair and all, by a bailiff.

VICTORIA BARRACKS

History presents arms at the main gateway of Victoria Barracks, in Oxford Street, Paddington. Here, twenty-four hours a day since 1848, sentries have been on duty in the sandstone guardroom. Inside, the original hand-hewn roof-beams, mellowed, but not fretted by time, cross swords.

The barracks were begun in 1836 to plans by Major George Barney. Wynyard Barracks, in George Street, the first in the colony, were decaying, and the sixteen acres on which they stood were coveted by merchants. To the chagrin of the military, the new site was out of town, set in a waste of dunes. Semi-exile, thought the authorities, would be good for discipline; softened by too close a contact with the heart of Sydney, soldiers had tended to become unruly.

Just before the first part of Victoria Barracks was opened, the 99th Duke of Edinburgh's (Wiltshire) Regiment was on the verge of mutiny in Wynyard Barracks. To take them out to the sandhills of Paddington might invite riot. So the 11th North Devonshires, fresh from service in Hobart, were marched into the new barracks while convict gangs building them toiled on. The barracks were magnificently constructed, but conditions could be hard for troops. A hated duty was windlassing water out of the barrack wells. At peril of their lives, two soldiers had to go down the wells to steer the great iron buckets.

The barracks housed famous British regiments until 1870, when Imperial troops withdrew. Since then they have been a Headquarters for Australian commands. Kept in the pink of preservation, the great sweep of pillared buildings, with the main block stretching 740 feet, is considered one of the best examples of colonial military architecture in the British Commonwealth. Certainly it is one of the finest historical sights in Sydney.

RICHMOND VILLA

For 126 years Richmond Villa, the prettiest old house in the city, sat snugly behind Parliament House. Then, in 1976-77, the villa was transported in its entirety to a new site in Kent Street, where it became the home of the Genealogical Society of New South Wales.

The original site of the Villa, facing the Domain, was part of a one-acre grant in Macquarie Street by Governor Macquarie to his dashing Irish Lieutenant-Governor, Maurice O'Connell. Later the land passed into other hands and was subdivided.

In 1849 three of the lots were sold to the Colonial Architect, Mortimer Lewis, who boldly made a breach in the Domain wall that sealed the property off from the park and started work on his fine gabled sandstone Gothic villa.

No better site could have been chosen for a man with a sociable nature, for the Domain had by then shed its character of official wilderness. This land, that Governor Phillip had dedicated as government property, not to be alienated, had for more than fifty years largely been a waste of scrubland, apart from the portion developed as Botanic Gardens.

In the 1840s it was put in order. A road that became a carriage drive for gentry was favoured for afternoon social and fashion parades. But Mortimer Lewis hardly stayed long enough to enjoy it all. He sold his house within a year of moving in. Various owners held it until it was acquired, by the state in 1879 and used as an annexe to Parliament House. For half a century, from 1922, it was also the headquarters of the Country Party of New South Wales.

ARGYLE PLACE

The old people of Miller's Point, drowsing in front of their hideous modern "amenities centre," have a view of something more in keeping with age. Before them, prim as an old-fashioned posy, exuding village-green charm, lies the city's last truly picturesque patch of its domestic past. A row of Georgian-type terraces and a cottage or two, framed like valentines in Victorian iron lace, face a tiny park of old trees.

Most of the houses were built in the decade 1840-50. For over a century nobody thought much about them. Then, in 1961, to the astonishment of the tenants (some families had lived there for four generations), their landlords, the Maritime Services Board, prodded by the National Trust, moved in with gallons of tastefully chosen paint. Furbished in soft colours, the iron lace crisped up with white, the old houses acquired a new status. This, citizens began to tell one another, was a part of old Sydney that it would be a crime to see swept away in the modernizing of the area, although there is a touch of irony in preserving anything so douce and respectable as the houses of Argyle Place as a symbol of The Rocks.

Behind them, tumbling down to the harbour's edge and spreading east, was the colony's first slum, a thieves' stew with a reputation as evil as its stench. Shanty houses stuck like wasps' nests to the precipitous rock slopes. Many were baited with grog and harlots for the worst element among the visiting seamen. There was no running water, no sanitation. Water had to be scooped out of rock seepage or bought by the bucket from a visiting carter. Goats swarmed the slimy paths; they were more numerous than the ragged children, but outnumbered by rats. Larrikin pushes terrorized the district toward the end of the century.

These memories pass like the shadow of a carrion crow across the smiling little square.

SYDNEY UNIVERSITY

Despite the claims of technologists, and the nightmarish jumble of buildings created on the site in the past twenty years, the heart of Sydney University remains its Gothic main Arts block and Great Hall. This was the finest work of Edmund Blacket, creator of St Andrew's Cathedral. The commission meant so much to him that he gave up his post as Colonial Architect in order to concentrate on it.

When Blacket designed the carved cedar ceiling of the Great Hall he had London's Westminster Hall in mind. And when he drew the Tudor perpendicular towers and pinnacles of the university, his spirit communed with the genius of English builders of the past. The gentle nature of the man shows charmingly in a story of how he celebrated his triumph of design. In 1855 the university Senate was due to attend the laying of the foundation stone by the Governor. The evening before the ceremony, Blacket took his wife Sarah, her sister, Mary Mease, and Mary's particular friend, Mary Stiles, to the site of the Great Hall. To the young ladies' joy they found that an unofficial stone, cut with their initials and the date, had by his order been laid in a corner of the future hall. (He had a fondness for carved initials. His own, *E.T.B.* may be seen at the side of the main entrance to the Hall.)

Blacket was a talented designer of stained glass; but he must have been relieved when craftsmen in England were given the huge job of creating the glass windows of the Great Hall, which celebrate the founders of Oxford and Cambridge colleges, and kings and queens of England.

After World War I, as a memorial to University dead, a carillon was installed in Blacket's graceful clock-tower. Concerts are occasionally given on it by official carillonists.

ST PHILIP'S CHURCH

The chaplain to the First Fleet, Richard Johnson, grieved by the secular spirit of Governor Phillip (who seemed to care more about food and shelter for his people than their souls), set about getting his own church built. A wattle-and-daub affair, costing about £40, it was set in the vicinity of the present Hunter Street. It lasted five years until it was burnt in 1798, probably by convicts in revenge for the way their rations were docked when they dodged Sunday services.

The first regular Anglican Church, St Phillip's (*double-ell*— named for the unchurchly Governor), was begun on Church Hill by Governor Hunter, who tacked an ugly building to a tall clock-tower used by the military as an observatory. The tower was knocked down twice by storms before the church was opened for worship in 1809. Other storms raged too; in 1808, long before the building was consecrated, it was used for a rowdy meeting of colonists planning to depose Governor Bligh.

Nobody seems to have been sorry when the barn-like old church gave way in 1856 to the new St Philip's (now spelt more appropriately to celebrate the saint). A tablet in Lang Park on Church Hill marks the site of the first church. The new one, placed further west, is one of the most admired works in Edmund Blacket's best Gothic style. The stained-glass windows he installed are particularly beautiful; being lightly tinted, they allow a soft brightness to illumine the interior, even on dull days.

St Philip's took eight years to complete. Fashionable Anglicans, no doubt depressed by the gloom and decay of the old church, preferred St James', down near Hyde Park. Funds were hard to raise. There was, moreover, a shortage of workmen. Unimpressed by the need for tributes to God, most of them had gone to work for mammon, on the goldfields.

FORT DENISON

For Governor Phillip the island off Farm Cove, a conical peak on an acre of stunted bush, had one function—as a dump, until he had time to build a gaol for convicts who committed crimes after reaching the colony. Marooned convicts, whose ration of bread and water was rowed to them once a week, changed its name from Rock Island to Pinchgut.

Sometimes the hangman went on the food boat. For years the remnants of a man's bones hung in chains on a gibbet on the island. Francis Morgan, convicted with others of the murder of a man on the North Shore, was strung up as a warning. There's a legend that, asked if he wished to make any last remark, he looked about him and said, "Well, you have here indeed a beautiful harbour."

Early in 1840, after two American warships had sneaked into the harbour at night without a pilot, Governor Gipps decided to erect a battery on the island. He set gangs of convicts to level the rock, and almost had the job done when he ran out of funds. The ruining of what had once been a lovely if sinister spot sent Dr Dunmore Lang into a rage. He denounced the "official Goth or Hun."

Military minds, however, could not resist the lure of the island. When there was a Russian invasion scare during the Crimean War a fort was built on it—a martello tower with outbuildings for powder magazines and quarters for a small permanent garrison. Foundations were quarried deep into the island rock. Stone for the 12-foot-thick walls was brought from Kurraba Point. The fort, completed in 1857, was named after the Governor, Sir William Denison.

The island is now used as a tide-gauge and light and fog signal station. Its one o'clock gun was discontinued in 1942.

THE OBSERVATORY

Visitors to the green hill of the Observatory have been known to decide with morbid relish that the chains hanging from the wall are relics of barbarous treatment of convicts. The truth is that they were used to brace the flagstaffs which stood here for more than a century. Their signals were the first main means of alerting the town that a ship had entered the Harbour. Governor Phillip's first fort stood here also, and the public windmills that ground the colonists' corn.

From the start, there has always been some work on astronomy in New South Wales, of varying efficiency, and on various sites. In 1857, under the Rev. W. Scott—our first professional astronomical observer, chosen by the Astronomer Royal—work began on the building that still stands on Observatory Hill. Scott's equipment and funds were meagre, but, like so many of his contemporaries, he did not aim to build only for his generation. His Florentine Renaissance observatory was intended to "satisfy all the astronomical requirements of the colony for the next century." It has not done that, but the fine stone monument to his breadth of vision is still a pleasure to look at, and has well served the purpose it has been chiefly used for since 1887—astrographic cataloguing. As part of a world scheme the Observatory from that year undertook to map three-quarters of a million stars in about a fifteenth of the sky. In spite of troubles caused by increasing city smog, the work was finished in 1962, and is now being revised.

In all its history there has been little excitement at the Observatory except for the day in 1877 when someone sent the director, Henry Russell, a bomb. Russell was not hurt, and nobody discovered why the attempt was made.

SYDNEY GRAMMAR SCHOOL

The first school to bear the name Sydney Grammar was an academy set up in 1825 by Dr Lawrence Halloran, a colourful character. He had served at Trafalgar as a chaplain and had carried his fighting qualities ashore to the extent of taking part in a duel. A talent for slanderous verse had involved him in a libel suit; and in 1818, when a country curate, he had pleaded guilty to counterfeiting a frank to the value of ten-pence, and had been transported for seven years. Despite his record, a number of leading families supported his Sydney Public Free Grammar School. If it hadn't been for his turbulent nature, the school might have been a success. But he talked his way into unpopularity, and his school closed in 1826.

Sydney Grammar had been undenominational. This idea had such an appeal that prominent citizens had soon arranged for a new school to be established on the same lines. A site was found alongside Hyde Park, and the foundation stone was laid in 1830. To avoid association with Dr Halloran's defunct establishment, it was called the Sydney College. After a chequered career it closed in 1847, land and buildings being sold to Sydney University.

By then there were several schools in Sydney run by churches. Some colonists deplored the sectarianism they feared these would breed, and the Hyde Park site was reacquired from the University. Edmund Blacket added to the buildings, in classical style, and the new Sydney Grammar opened in 1857. After some troubles it settled down to become one of the most famous private schools in Australia. Grammar is cramped for grounds, but its stately facade on College Street matches well with its neighbour, the Museum.

THE G.P.O.

Rearing itself honey-pale above the grimy fabric beneath, the G.P.O. clock-tower represents a triumph of public sentiment over utility. In 1942 the 51-year-old tower, because of a fear that it would act as a landmark for Japanese raiders, was dismantled and sent packing, with its great clock and chime of five bells, to a government store.

After the war, as costs went up, officialdom began to hedge about restoring the tower and clock. To their astonishment, a public grievance began to smoulder, flaring in bursts of resentment in the columns of the papers. Seventeen years later, bureaucracy capitulated. It took a year's expert jigsaw work and £93,000 of public money to staunch the citizens' nostalgia. But when the chimes of the G.P.O. clock boomed out again for the first time, on Anzac Day 1964, the city seemed to give a sigh of triumph. Few of those who pass along Martin Place now bother to raise their eyes to the clock, but it is enough to know from its voice that it is back. It now strikes only the daylight hours; it is too loud for city sleepers.

Since the battle of the tower was fought and won, a thin note of uncertainty has diluted the demands of the realists that the whole inefficient, uncomfortable, outmoded pile of the G.P.O. should be razed, and something in keeping with the twentieth century put in its place. For who will now dare lay the first finger on this massive heap of Victorianism, begun in 1874 to replace the original Sydney Post Office? The sculptured heads of anonymous queens along the façade frown defiance. And, around on the Pitt Street façade, the stone effigy of James Barnet, the building's architect, in his niche among a delightful frieze of colonial figures, looks remarkably smug.

THE ART GALLERY

"New South Wales," a wag wrote in 1871, "is doing as well as can be expected so far as shop-keeping and squatting are concerned; the vile bodies of its inhabitants are well provided for, but the mind, the soul, is starved and fossilized. . . ." He suggested that the new N.S.W. Academy of Art—Society for the Promotion of the Study of the Various Departments of the Fine Arts and for Periodical Exhibitions of Works of Art in Sydney—might fill the gap. So for about nine years genteel society rallied to the Academy's functions, held in a hired hall. Art works were exhibited, and were sometimes raffled in an Art Union (a word that survives to describe inartistic charity lotteries).

The Academy gradually faded out, but it led to the formation of a state Art Gallery. The first collection made by this body, housed in a dancing academy, opened in 1876. Later it spent some time in the International Exhibition building on Figtree Avenue. In 1885 it moved to six rooms (referred to in the Press as a "shelter shed") in the beginnings of the present building in the Domain. What is now a respectable classical façade was adapted from an earlier, hideous design. A set of indifferent bronze reliefs commemorating various artists was, perhaps fortunately, never carried through.

Feeble attempts to enlarge the Gallery's cramped and rundown quarters were made from time to time in the twentieth century but mainly foundered for lack of funds, a chronic ailment still. But as part of the Captain Cook Bi-Centenary celebrations the government raised the money for a new wing in modern style, opened in 1972. The new blends quietly enough with the old.

THE CUSTOMS HOUSE

Probably the oddest event in which Sydney's Customs men ever took part occurred when, in 1836, at the request of John Tawell, they rowed more than 500 gallons of rum and gin out into Sydney Cove, stove the casks in, and poured the spirit into the Harbour.

Tawell, an emancipated forger who had become a Quaker, was demonstrating his sincerity to a visiting leader of the sect, James Backhouse, and was sacrificing a cargo he had imported for profit. Backhouse reported: "We were much pleased with the hearty manner in which the Customs house officers superintended the sacrifice of property to principle." (Tawell later fell from grace, poisoned his mistress, and was executed.)

In those days, Customs officers were lodged near the Argyle Cut, among the colony's most dedicated smugglers. In the 1840s they moved to a drab building on the present site at Circular Quay, where, it is almost agreed, the First Fleeters raised the first flag. In the 1880s and 1890s the Customs House was elaborated into a U-shape, swallowing most of the old building, and the coat-of-arms over the entrance, one of the best stone carvings in Australia, was added. In 1917 the interior courtyard was roofed and converted to offices. Today, the Customs House is the only thing that adds historical dignity to Circular Quay, although its tawny sandstone lacks the patina of age. (An expert on old buildings recently complained that it was being "steam-cleaned out of existence.")

When Captain John Piper was Controller of Customs he allowed merchants to pay duty on credit. Governor Darling suspended him, and asked him to account for thousands of pounds uncollected. Captain Piper had himself rowed to the Heads, where he cast himself into what he announced would be a watery grave. His servants rescued him, spoiling his gesture.

ACKNOWLEDGMENTS

The author's thanks are especially due to Miss Rachel Roxburgh, of the Historic Buildings Committee of the National Trust of Australia (N.S.W.), and Mr Alec Chisholm, O.B.E., of the Royal Historical Society of Australia, who read and commented on the manuscript; to the Trustees of the Public Library of N.S.W., for permission to consult material in the Mitchell Library; to the Principal Archivist of the Archives Office of N.S.W., for information supplied from the State Archives; the Trustees of the Art Gallery of N.S.W., for permission to consult library material and records; the General Officer Commanding Eastern Command, Maj.-General T. J. Daly, for permission to read a paper on the history of Victoria Barracks; Mr W. Crisp, former Principal, East Sydney Technical College, for information on the history of Darlinghurst Gaol; the Librarian, Sydney Grammar School; Mr Murray Tyrrell, Press Officer, Government House, Canberra, A.C.T., for information on the history of Admiralty House; Mr Peter Collis, Public Relations Officer, Australian Museum; the Rev. A. C. H. Yuill, Th.L., Rector of Holy Trinity, Miller's Point; Father E. Kelly, S.M., of St Patrick's, Church Hill, Sydney.

56

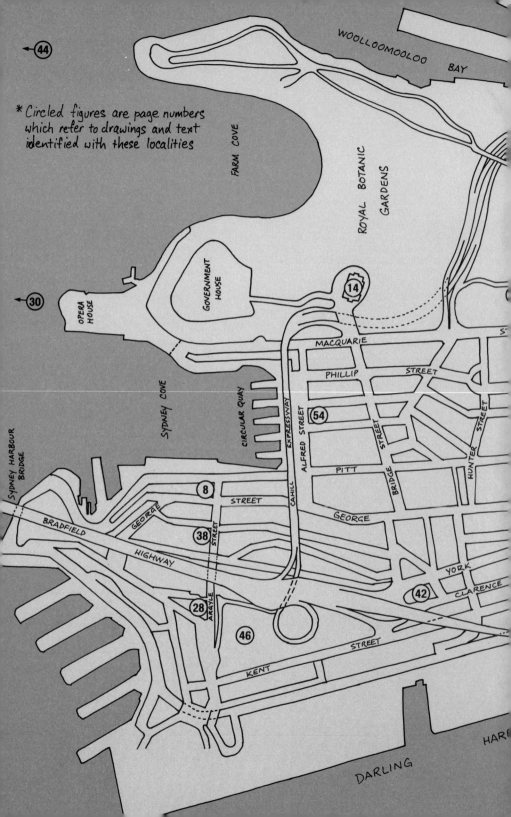

* Circled figures are page numbers which refer to drawings and text identified with these localities